HOW TO SURVIVE THE 6TH GRADE

Written By

J. R. Clark

ISBN: 978-0-578-98811-5

Words of Heart
New York, NY

Cover Illustration, Cover Design, and Interior layout
by Tami Boyce (tamiboyce.com)

This one is for all the people
who made this dream become reality.
To my husband Howard, my daughter Ashtyn,
my son Little Howie, my parents, and my brother EJ—
who have supported me since Day 1,
To Mom, her best friend Miss Tami, and my friend
Jem—who read all versions of the book and who
pressed me to keep writing in spite of the many
changes that needed to happen,
To Whelan, Fisher, Williamson, Tylaiah, and KJ —
who took time from their busy lives to read the book,
give feedback, and encourage me to publish,
To Ms. Tami Boyce, who stuck with me through all of
my self-doubt, and who created the beautiful book
cover and formatted the book for me,
And to me, who didn't give up:
Congratulations!
May this book help change the world we live in.

TABLE OF CONTENTS

STEP ONE:

Look Below the Surface

When I first got the acceptance letter to Live Oak Middle Magnet STEM School in the mail, I almost fainted. I had begged Mama to let me apply to that school after seeing a commercial for it on television. "Live Oak Middle Magnet STEM School," the man in the commercial had said, "...is the place where every child's dreams come true!" I was a child, and I had dreams, so the school sounded perfect.

Mama and Daddy took a day off from their jobs to take me to orientation. I remember that I hopped into Daddy's black Expedition with the eagerness of a kid waiting to open up presents on Christmas Day. For the entire ride to the school, I asked question after question: "Mama, do you think the walls are as white there as they were on TV? Daddy, do you think my teachers will be as nice as the ones I have now?"

As soon as we pulled into the parking lot, my jaw dropped. I had never, ever seen a school as beautiful as Live Oak. It was surrounded by tall oak trees, a really neat lawn, and beautiful shrubs with white flowers in them. As we walked through the school, I marveled at how clean the walkway was: not even a piece of gum stained the concrete! And in the middle of the school was a beautiful courtyard. It looked like paradise.

Mama told me to keep my options open. "Now you know you applied to two other schools, and with your grades, I'm sure you'll be able to get into those schools as well. Let's just wait before we make a decision," she said. But the decision was already made in my mind. I fell in love with Live Oak the minute I stepped onto the campus, and there was no way anyone would be able to convince me otherwise.

The summer of 2018 was the longest summer of my life. But when the first day of school finally came in August, I was ready. I had already stuffed my backpack with notebooks, binders, and papers for each subject. My First Day of School outfit, a burgundy flare dress with gray tights, had already been ironed and creased to perfection. And Mama had already flat ironed my hair. That morning, as I glanced at my reflection in the mirror—making sure there was no cold in my eyes or boogers in my nose—I smiled. "You look good, girl," I told myself. I felt as ready and as excited as ever!

My feelings of excitement multiplied as I traveled from classroom to classroom that day.

My history teacher, Mr. Manor, was so cool. He stood in front of us, on the first day of school, wearing jeans. "I'm laid back and I like to have fun," he had said, "But don't try me." In math class, Mrs. James went over the rules and expectations for work. She talked about how much of a stickler she was for neatness. She then had us do some math problems, and she actually showed my work to the rest of the class! "Your work should be as neat and organized as Ashley's," she had said. As I watched the rest of the class stare at my paper, I couldn't help but smile. My head swelled to the size of a watermelon.

In every classroom, I felt challenged—which was so different from elementary school, where things came so easily for me. I was in a new world, and I absolutely adored it.

This feeling lasted all the way until lunchtime. When the lunch bell rang, I crossed the school's courtyard to the cafeteria. Upon opening the door, my senses were overwhelmed with the smell of lasagna and the loud, high-pitched voices of excited students. I quickly learned that my school's cafeteria was where all the action happened. It was the place where people met their friends—catching up on the latest gossip. It was where kids got to show off their brand new outfits and sneakers. It was the one time of day when kids from all grades gathered together. And it was the one place in the entire school where kids didn't have to answer questions about history or math. For these reasons, every kid loved going to lunch.

Every kid, that is, except me.

Seeing my cafeteria at lunchtime reminded me of the day Mama taught me how to do laundry. "Make sure you carefully separate the clothes. We don't want the colors mixed in with the whites because it'll ruin them, and then I'll have to buy new white clothes," she had said. To make sure I knew how serious she was, she added her infamous warning: "And you know money doesn't grow on trees!"

And as I gazed out at the scene in my cafeteria on the first day of school, I realized that laundry wasn't the only thing that people sorted. My cafeteria was sorted by race.

At the tables closest to the doors were all of the cool girls. Some of them had blonde hair, some had red hair, and others had brown hair. But all of them were white.

Next to them were the cool boys—the ones who came to school in Guess jeans and expensive Nikes. They were popular, and everybody wanted to be their friends. But every single boy at those tables was white too.

On the opposite side of the cafeteria were the Black kids. I scanned that area to look for an empty seat. I spotted a table where other girls, who looked like me, were sitting. They weren't talking—just quietly eating lunch. *Maybe they don't know each other very well,* I thought. *This is perfect.*

I started inching toward the table I had spotted with my black lunchbox in tow. To get to the table, I had to walk past the cool girls' and cool boys' tables. As I squeezed in between the seats, I accidentally stumbled into one of the girls. She was a tall girl with long blonde hair that draped across her back.

"I'm so sorry," I said. I started to walk away, but the girl reached out for me.

"Wait," the girl said, "I don't remember seeing you before. What's your name?"

"I'm Ashley," I said. "What's your name?"

"You don't know *my* name?" She glanced at her friends and they started snickering. Then she looked back at me. "Just watch where you are going next time."

"It was an accident," I said, as I rolled my eyes. "That's why I said 'I'm sorry.'"

"Sure it was, Chia Pet," she said. The table roared with laughter.

As I walked away, I was so confused. *What's a Chia Pet? And why was that blonde girl so angry with me for accidentally bumping into her?* I wondered.

When I finally reached the table in the "Black section," it turned out that I was right. The girls there were all sixth graders and didn't know anyone. I tried to get to know them, but I could barely focus. The blonde girl's words were still echoing in my head: "Sure it was, Chia Pet," she had said. *Why was that so funny?*

Once I arrived home, it took me about 30 seconds to figure out what the blonde girl had meant. I opened my laptop, typed "Chia Pet" into the search bar, clicked on images, and immediately gasped. A Chia Pet was a small figurine, and each one I saw had green, bushy leaves for hair. It had dawned on me that the blonde girl was teasing me about my hair.

In horror, I ran to the bathroom and looked in the mirror. Just as I had suspected, my hair had left its flat-ironed, straightened state and returned to its natural kinks and coils. Without my permission, my hair had shrunken back up into an almost-afro.

I suddenly felt ugly.

At dinnertime, my parents asked me about how the first day of school went. I told them about each class and how much fun I had. I told them that I met new girls at lunchtime. But I didn't tell them about the blonde girl. I didn't want my parents to overreact—as they often did. But mostly, *I* wanted to handle it. I wanted to show those girls exactly who they were messing with.

As I went to sleep that night, I said my prayers and made a silent vow: I would confront that girl tomorrow, and I would let her know exactly who I am.

STEP TWO:

Know Yourself

In elementary school, I was one of the most popular girls in school. Teachers knew me for being smart and hard-working and kids knew me for being funny and kind. No one knew, though, that I had a different side to me. If ever someone pushed me, I would push back. And I would push back much harder than they did.

I first met this other side at my Grandpa's funeral three years ago—when I saw my cousin Erica for the first time. She was older than me, and I was hoping that I could look up to her.

But it only took a few seconds for me to realize that she was a bad apple. During the funeral, she had the nerve to sit next to me on the church pew—blowing chewing gum bubbles. The whole time the preacher talked, she kept blowing bubbles and popping them. Her mom, my Auntie Sarah, was too upset about Grandpa's death to notice, but even at the age of 8, I knew that no one should have gum in church. As soon as Erica blew another bubble, I elbowed her and whispered as viciously as I could: "Stop blowing bubbles in church." She looked at me and rolled her eyes. But she didn't blow another bubble.

Since then, I knew I had to make sure I kept my temper under control so that I didn't get in trouble. But I also knew there were times when I needed to let people know I had another side to me. And this was one of those times.

As I got dressed for the second day of school, I silently reflected on the plan I had come up with for the girl, whom I nicknamed "Blondie."

First, I would walk up to her at lunch and ask her if I could talk to her privately. Once we started talking, I would firmly tell her that I didn't like her comment about my hair. If she started to argue with me, I would interrupt her and warn her that if she ever even looked my way again, she would be sorry.

Mama interrupted my thoughts. "Ash, do you want to pull your hair back into a ponytail? Or do you want to wear it out?"

I looked in the mirror at my hair. By now, it had completely reverted to an afro. I looked at my black coils, and Blondie's words returned to my ears.

"I'll slick it back," I said. I pulled my hair back into a frizzy ponytail and secured it with a scrunchie. Then, I threw a cute bucket hat on.

Mama flashed me a look. "Will your teachers let you wear that hat all day?"

"Yes, Mama. I don't think they'll mind."

"Well, if you have to take it off, you better not lose it. You know money doesn't grow on trees!"

I was on autopilot for the entire morning until lunchtime—when I knew I would have to confront Blondie. Just like the day before, the lunchroom was abuzz with excitement. I slid past two people doing a secret handshake, meandered through a few cool kids' tables, and then made my way to Blondie. Her blonde hair was tied into a high ponytail with a blue ribbon around it. She was laughing with the other girls at her table about something that probably wasn't even funny.

"Excuse me," I said when I reached my destination. I was met with disapproving eyes and divided attention. "I'm Ashley. We met yesterday-" I started.

Blondie interrupted me. "We know who you are. What do you want?"

I looked at Blondie. Her blue eyes looked like daggers. But I was determined not to back down.

"I want to talk to you about yesterday. Can I talk to you privately?" I asked.

The girl stood up. "You can talk to me right here," she said as she crossed her arms.

I knew she was only a few inches taller than me, but at that moment, it seemed like she was a giant. It also seemed to get quieter. I looked around and realized that we suddenly had an audience. Every kid in the area was staring at me—waiting to see how I would respond. *Stick to the script,* I told myself. *Stick to the script!*

I started talking, but I could barely recognize my voice. "Yesterday, you called me a Chia Pet," I said shakily. I heard a few snickers from the audience, and I became angry again. "I didn't appreciate that. You were talking about my hair, and that was a racist thing to say."

I didn't plan to say the word racist; it just fell out of my mouth. But it felt good that I had taken it there. After all, her comment felt like an attack on my hair—my *Black* hair.

Blondie's eyes grew wide. "Racist... I wasn't being–"

Another blonde girl at the table jumped up and cut her off.

"Don't let her bully you!" she said to Blondie. "Let her know exactly who you are."

Blondie paused, swallowed hard, and then started speaking again. "I think you're just jealous that your hair doesn't look like this," she said. On *this,* she whipped her long ponytail from side to side, as if her name was Willow Smith. And in the process, the tip of her ponytail touched my face—right above my lip.

Later, several kids would tell me that everyone burst out laughing. However, I didn't realize that at the time. I didn't hear the laughter and I didn't see the kids around me anymore. All I saw was red.

I grabbed her ponytail and yanked it so hard that she fell to the ground. Then I took my hat off and threw it in her face. "HOW DOES IT FEEL TO HAVE SOMETHING FLUNG IN *YOUR* FACE?" I yelled at the top of my lungs.

That morning, I had planned to simply confront Blondie so that we could move forward, but as the cafeteria monitors pulled me away from her, I knew something much bigger had started. As I looked into the faces of the rest of the girls at that table, I knew that this was an official declaration of war. And I secretly wondered how I would survive this school year.

STEP THREE:

Apologize When You're Wrong

"You know I raised you better than this!" Mama ranted, as we entered her red Toyota Camry. "I had to cancel my afternoon appointment to come out here to get you, and you know money doesn't grow on trees."

I finished the end of Mama's sentence, and I could tell that Mama was annoyed. But I heard her say that same phrase almost everyday. If she were me, she would be able to finish the sentence too.

"Little girl, don't play with me," she uttered through clenched teeth. Then she said the most dreadful words a child could ever hear: "You are in BIG trouble."

I could literally feel my body shaking. I hated my mom's punishments.

"Mama, you haven't even let me explain," I pleaded. "That girl flipped her hair at me and it hit me. She did it on purpose!"

"Ashley, this is the second day of school!" Mama declared. "How did it even get to this point?"

"Mama, I already told you what happened. She called me a Chia Pet. She was talking about my hair and I felt like she was being racist. And when I told this to the principal, he didn't even listen."

Dr. Johnson, my principal, seemed very nice at first, but when I explained why I had grabbed Blondie's hair and pushed her to the floor, he refused to accept my excuse. "We have a zero tolerance policy for violence of any kind, Ms. Woods," he had said to me. "You cannot go around being violent with everyone who teases you about your hair. You must learn how to ignore people. This type of behavior is unacceptable."

Dr. Johnson's words had stung. I knew that I was wrong for how I handled that situation. I had even understood why I needed to be suspended. But I had expected my principal to understand my pain. I had expected him to understand that Blondie's comment was deeper than teasing. And I had expected him to tell me that my anger made sense. He never did.

Mama didn't either. "Ashley, I have told you time and time again that the facts don't matter when race is involved. When a Black girl puts her hands on a white girl, no one wants to hear what you have to say. They automatically think that you're wrong and that you're a threat—whether you are or not!"

"Mama, it's not 1950," I retorted. "Things are different now. We just had a Black president for God's sake."

Wrong choice of words.

Mama was not pleased. I could tell because when she got mad, her Southern accent—that she usually disguised—emerged.

She responded, "See—that's the problem with the Black folk of today. No one can tell y'all anything because y'all think y'all know everything. But I got something that'll fix that problem. I'll show you when we get home."

For the rest of the ride home, I was silent. The lump in my throat was the size of a baseball.

• • •

For the most part, my mother was the ideal mom: she was nice, smart, and funny. But when she got upset, thunderstorm clouds appeared, and it rained cats and dogs. So, I really wasn't surprised when she announced that I was grounded for three weeks.

The only part of the whole punishment that got under my skin was what she did after she grounded me. She announced that she was going to the store to get dinner, and I automatically assumed she was going to get something healthy. When she returned, though, she had two liters of Coca Cola and a Meat Lovers pizza, which was my favorite.

"I'm not hungry," I told her when she came into my room with the pizza box.

I wasn't ready to kiss and make up. Mama's smile turned upside down.

"Ashley, I don't like to punish you, but you have to understand that I know what's best for you." I turned my face away from her, and she sat down on my bed. "Have you paid attention to the news at all lately?" she asked.

Mama knew that I had. "How could I not? You make me watch the news every night before I go to bed," I said.

"So you should know that unarmed Black people are being killed."

"Yes. I do know that. But what does that have to do with this situation?"

Mama went into a history lesson. "Being Black is a wonderful thing. But lies about Black people were created and carried through the media to make us look bad. These lies have criticized every part of us: our bodies, our minds, our intelligence, and our behavior. Throughout history, Black people have been compared to animals. We've been called dumb and ugly, and we have been called violent. We've been called these things so much that many people have started to believe these lies—without even knowing they believe them."

Mama paused to let her words seep in, and deep down I knew she was right. I had read books about some of these lies—books that described Black people as bad. I had spent my entire elementary experience learning about the white heroes who shaped America in the classroom while learning about Black heroes at home. I knew that the world I lived in wasn't right, but I was still confused about why Mama was bringing this up now.

She placed her hand on mine. "Some officers have shot Black people because they believe the lies and are therefore afraid of us. And these lies have not only affected police officers and their judgment—but also the judgment and perception of teachers, politicians, and even kids. You, my dear, are smart, beautiful, and strong. But the minute you put your hands on that girl, the only thing people saw was an angry Black girl. Your act today perpetuated the stereotype. And I know you had a reason to be upset, but unfortunately, we aren't given many chances to show who we are."

I stared at her. "So what am I supposed to do next time? Just walk away and let Blondie win?"

"Do you feel like you won anything today?"

I shook my head. I started thinking about those kids' faces as the cafeteria monitor walked me to the principal's office. They were looking at me with disgust. Though it felt good to put Blondie in her place, I knew that this conflict was far from over.

"Exactly," Mom said. "I'm not telling you to walk away and do nothing. I'm telling you to be the change you want to see. And until the change happens, you have to let me help you. You can't fight every problem on your own."

Deep down, I knew Mama was right. Before Mama came to school today, I was facing three full days of out-of-school suspension. But after Mama marched into the principal's office and pointed out that Blondie's hair flip was the inciting incident, my sentence was reduced. Now, Blondie and I both had one day of in-school suspension, and we had to write each other letters about how sorry we were and how we would always respect each other in the future. I knew that if Mama hadn't shown up, I would've been in major trouble.

Mama could tell I was processing this information. So she decided to place the cherry on the sundae.

"Baby, I'm sorry if it seemed like I wasn't on your side. But I want you to stop and think before you respond. Think about the consequences. Think about the message your actions are sending. Now let's eat this food before it gets cold."

We took our places at the kitchen table and devoured a total of four slices. I actually wanted more since I hadn't eaten lunch, but Mama wanted to be sure that Daddy had enough to eat when he got home. When he got home, though, he didn't even eat. He immediately started in on me.

"Ashley, what happened in school today?"

My mother, whose name has never been Ashley a day in her life, told Daddy the whole story.

Daddy finally turned to me. "Ashley," he said, "You're going to have to learn to control your temper. That's not how a Woods acts."

Once again, my mother replied, "I told her that she's grounded for three weeks. I want her to understand that she can't treat people any way she wants to just because she's angry."

Because I really wasn't a part of the conversation anyway, I used my homework as an excuse to leave the table. On my way to the room, Daddy yelled, "Don't forget to write that apology letter."

I didn't want to remember, but I knew I had to uphold my end of the bargain. So, in fat lettering on a piece of notebook paper, I wrote the following:

Dear Blondie,

Sorry for throwing you to the ground and throwing my hat at you. I wish this never happened. But hopefully, we can move past this.

Sincerely,
Ashley

Before I went to sleep that night, I made another silent vow to be the change and fix the situation with Blondie. I didn't know how I could fix it, but I knew that I had to try.

STEP FOUR:

Be the Change You Want to See

I woke up the next morning refreshed and optimistic. I was hopeful that my apology note and my determination to be kind to everyone would make a difference. But by lunchtime, I realized that things had gotten worse.

The cafeteria was still divided as it had always been. But as I made my way to my table, I saw some entirely different interactions between kids. Kids were bumping into each other without even saying sorry, and people from all sides of the cafeteria were scowling at each other. War had definitely started.

I made my way to my table—coaching myself the entire way: *Don't make eye contact, don't get angry, make it to your table. Don't make eye contact, don't get angry, make it to your table.*

But Blondie's voice pierced through my thoughts. I knew she was talking loudly on purpose; I knew she wanted me to hear what she was saying. And so, I started listening.

"Can you believe her? She actually wrote me an apology note that said she wanted us to move past this."

Another girl sitting at her table chimed in: "What? Like you would really want to talk to her again—after she attacked you and called *you* the racist? Please."

Blondie responded: "Yeah... she's dumb if she thinks I'm going to forgive her."

The other girl then said, "Wait, aren't they ALL dumb?"

The entire table erupted in laughter. I was livid. I wanted to go over to the table, knock the table down, and tell all of those girls off—one by one. But my mom's words echoed in my head: *Be the change you want to see.* So I exhaled, walked to my seat, and started opening my lunchbox. Just as I was about to take a bite from my sandwich, someone tapped me on the shoulder.

"Hey. My name is Ben. I just wanted to tell you that you were so brave yesterday."

I looked up to see who was speaking to me. A tall Hispanic boy with perfect teeth smiled at me. His hair was brown and curly—almost like mine. He had on a polo shirt and some jeans. I was not in the mood to talk, but I knew that a good conversation might be the very thing to distract me from getting into more trouble.

"Hi, Ben," I said. "Thank you. Do you want to sit and eat with me?"

Ben's eyes widened and he started to stutter. "I can't sit over here. Are you kidding me?" His eyes roamed across the cafeteria, and I suddenly realized what he meant. The kids that looked like him were sitting in the section in the very back of the cafeteria. He would be betraying his friends—and the entire social order at Live Oak—if he sat with me.

I lowered my head. "Oh, I understand," I said.

"I didn't mean to offend you," Ben said. "I just can't afford to make things any worse right now. I'll talk to you later."

I watched Ben walk away on what was the worst day of my life. Not only did I have beef with a whole group of girls for simply standing up for myself, but I was also stuck at my lunch table for the rest of the year. I didn't have one thing in common with the girls that sat at my table, except my race. I had no problem hanging with them; I just wanted the freedom to choose my friends. I wanted the freedom to sit somewhere else. I wanted these dumb restrictions that we had created to be eliminated. Before I realized it, a tear trickled down my face.

One of the girls I sat with, Brittany, started speaking: "Don't cry. Don't worry about those girls. They're just stupid."

Another girl named Tasha chimed in: "Yeah, girl. We saw what you did yesterday, but stop trying so hard. This is just the way things are. It's not a big deal. We just need to know our place."

I smiled at them. I knew they were just trying to console me. But deep within my heart, I knew two things. One, I knew that this *was* a big deal—even if no one else realized it. And two, I knew I would help things change at this school. Very soon.

STEP FIVE:

Know That Things Can Always Be Worse

My first week in middle school had been absolutely horrible. Each lunch session, the cool girls would have a fresh insult for me. They would call me "ugly" as I walked by—making fun of my hair and my outfits. Or they would simply flash me dirty looks. And when Dr. Johnson finally handed me Blondie's "apology" note, I discovered why: she believed everything was my fault. "I didn't even touch you on purpose, but you decided to put your hands on me," she had written. "And you did it in front of the whole cafeteria. I will never forgive you."

By Friday, I thought that things could not get any worse. But on Saturday morning, my life took a plunge.

It all started with one phone call from Grandma. Mama usually loved talking to Grandma, but shortly after taking the phone call in her room, I heard Mama scream. Five minutes later, Mama came into my room with tear-stained cheeks.

"Auntie Sarah is dead," she managed to say before bursting into tears.

Although Mama and Auntie Sarah were close, they were completely different. Auntie Sarah had gold teeth in her mouth; Mama would die before she did anything to her teeth. Auntie Sarah had at least ten tattoos. Mama had no tattoos. Auntie Sarah thought green was an acceptable hair color; Mama was hesitant to give her clients brown highlights. The two were polar opposites.

Still, Auntie Sarah was Mama's younger sister, and Mama loved her to pieces. I knew Mama was hurting, but I didn't really know what to say.

"The cancer came back," Mama said. "And it was too late to stop it."

Auntie Sarah had been diagnosed with stomach cancer years ago. About two years ago, she had announced to us that the cancer had gone into remission. I had assumed that it was gone by now, but I was obviously wrong.

"What's going to happen to Erica?" I asked.

Mama started crying harder. "Erica's birthday is in three months, Ash. Three months! And now Auntie Sarah's gone. Erica's all alone in the world."

Erica was supposed to turn 16 in November—a week before Thanksgiving. I remembered that Auntie Sarah had mentioned that she was planning a Sweet 16 party for her.

But now, that wouldn't happen. And because her father wasn't in her life, Erica had no one to take care of her.

Daddy came into the room and hugged Mama. "Ashley, we need to talk to you," he said.

I swallowed hard. Anytime my parents said the words "We need to talk to you," something big was happening. The last time they said that, they thought Mama was pregnant. It ended up being gas.

Daddy spoke. "Erica is going to need love and support during this time. She's going to need a family. And so we agreed to let her come and live with us. She will be like a big sister to you. She's going to move into the guest room."

My jaw dropped. I understood that this was a difficult time for Erica, but my parents knew how I felt about her. *How could they agree to something like this without talking to me first?*

"Daddy," I pleaded. "Why does she have to stay here? There are other places she can go."

Daddy raised his eyebrows and asked me where my cousin could live. I was glad to provide my suggestions: "The homeless shelter; old, abandoned buildings; with another relative-"

Mama cut my litany short. "Ashley, stop being so ridiculous. All Erica needs is love and support."

I sighed. Just when I had thought things couldn't get any worse, they did. I was so ready for this year to end.

I looked at my parents. "Okay," I said. "I know Erica is going through a difficult time, so I'm going to try to be there for her."

Mama and Daddy hugged me. "It won't be as bad as you think," Daddy said.

"Yes," Mama said as she gently squeezed my hand. "You girls will get along. I promise you that."

STEP SIX:

Be Nice, Even When It Hurts

Too bad we didn't make a wager to Mom's promise. The minute Erica walked into the house, we started arguing.

I wanted her to keep her hair products in the guest room; she wanted to clutter my bathroom counter with gel, spritz, combs, and brushes.

"You don't even have that much hair!" I yelled—referring to her short haircut with shaved sides.

She jumped down my throat: "See, that's why I didn't want to stay with your STUCK UP BUTT!"

I was about to tell her that I wasn't stuck up and that *she* was the real problem here, but Mama pulled me away from her. "You girls need to stop it! Y'all are just going to have to find a way to get along."

"How can I get along with *that*?" I asked between angry, audible breaths. Mama pinched my ear and led me into the dining room.

"Ashley, you need to chill out. I know she's different from you, but you're just going to have to learn how to like her. My sister and I were different, but we got along."

I pointed out the fact that I wasn't Erica's sister, so Mama tried a different approach.

"Well how about this?" she hissed. "If you don't try to get along with her, you're going to have to deal with your father." That was all she needed to say. As big as Daddy was, I didn't want to have to face him. So, I acquiesced.

We returned to find Erica's hair products all over the bathroom. Mama helped her place the products in the cabinet and told her to make herself at home. Then, Mama left the two of us alone.

Mama's threat echoed in my head, so I asked the only question I could think of that was nice: "What do you like to do?"

Erica rolled her eyes. "Don't try it. I know you don't like me, and I hate fake people."

"Well, then I won't talk to you at all," I said—rolling my eyes in the process.

"Fine!"

We went into our respective rooms, slammed the doors, and occupied ourselves. Since I couldn't watch tv, I pulled out some old books. It had been a while since I read *The Westing Game*, one of my favorite books. As soon as I flipped the page to the second chapter, I heard a strange sound coming from the guest room. I rushed into the room—only to find Erica edging the back of her hair with clippers. Little pieces of orange fuzz were all over the floor.

"What are you doing?" I cried as I rushed toward her.

"What does it look like?"

I stared at Erica's orange hair. I guess it was supposed to be blonde, but whoever did her hair didn't leave the tint on long enough. She looked like a pumpkin. Erica needed immediate assistance, and I knew just the person who would help.

"Erica, my mom does hair for a living," I said. "Why don't you go and ask her to fix your hair?"

You would've thought I told this girl that she was the reason Aretha Franklin died. She whipped around, and with wide eyes, accused me of insulting her. "What are you trying to say?"

I took a deep breath. "Erica," I said, "it just doesn't make any sense to be in here cutting your hair when you now live with a hair professional. Just ask my mom to help you fix it!"

Erica was surprisingly quiet as she followed me to my parents' room. I knocked on the door and went in after they answered. They were sitting on the bed watching tv.

"Mama," I said, "Erica needs you to fix her hair. Can you help it or is it too far gone?"

I must've said the last part with a terrible look on my face because Daddy said his famous phrase: "Ashley, that's not how a Woods acts."

Mama got out of the bed and examined Erica's hair closely. Then, she told us to go into the den and wait for her.

Mama used to do hair at the house, but after she realized she could make more money by owning a salon, she bought a building and hired some employees. Since Mama never changed the den back into a family room, it still looked like a mini hair salon with hair dryers and washing sinks.

I took Erica to the back of the house and turned on the lights. Erica sat in the chair and looked in the mirror. She stared at herself for a while, and then tears started falling. I thought she was tough, so the tears shocked me.

"What's wrong?" I asked.

"I don't know. I guess I miss my mom," she said while wiping her tears.

I didn't know what to say. I had spent so much time thinking about how much I didn't like Erica that I hadn't even thought about how I could make her feel better. I wanted to say something that would make her feel happy. I just couldn't find the words.

Mama saved the day.

"Erica, your mom was one special lady," Mama said as she gave Erica a hug. "I was very nervous as a child and I was careful about everything I said and did, but your mom—she taught me how to live. She said whatever came to her mind, and she didn't mind confronting anybody who disrespected her. She was so brave and even though I was older, I always looked up to her for that."

As she worked the shampoo into Erica's hair, she started telling Erica stories about her mom. I sat in another chair and listened. Some of the stories were funny and made us laugh—like when Auntie Sarah hit this boy for calling Mama a banana because she had on yellow tights. Some of the stories were sad. But as Mama's hands worked on Erica's hair, her words worked on Erica's heart.

"Wow," Erica exclaimed as she looked in the mirror after Mama had finished curling her hair. "I look good," she said.

Mama smiled and gave her another hug. "You do look good," Mama said. "Now go and finish unpacking."

When Erica left the room, Mama turned to me. "See," she said.

"See what?"

"Erica is not a bad person. She's in pain. And what she needs from you is understanding, not criticism."

"I still don't like her," I said. But when Mama shot me a look, I added: "But I guess I can be nicer."

"Thank you! That's all I'm asking you to do!" Mama said as she grabbed my hand. We walked out of the den, turned out the light, and closed the door. I didn't know how I was going to be nicer, but I was definitely going to try. Once again, I silently hoped that this year didn't get any worse.

STEP SEVEN:

Ask For What You Want

I used to wonder what it would be like to have a sibling. When I was younger, I would beg Mama and Daddy to have another child.

"I need someone to play with," I would demand in my high-pitched voice.

Daddy's answer would always be, "If God permits."

But as I looked over the past two months that Erica had been with us, I wished God never permitted. I suddenly learned what siblings came with, and I didn't like it at all.

When Daddy brought home treats now, I had to share them. When Mama went shopping, she had to buy clothes for both Erica and me. When we had family dinner conversations, I was no longer the center of attention. I had to share the spotlight with Erica, and she talked entirely too much. Sometimes, she took over our entire dinner conversation. My life, as I had known it, had completely changed the minute Erica walked through the door.

When I brought home my report card on Halloween, I was sure that I was going to get my usual reward. Daddy always gave me five dollars per A I earned. Since I made all As for that nine-week period, I thought I was going to get 35 dollars. What I got instead was a measly 14 dollars.

"What happened, daddy?" I asked. "You can see that I made seven As. That means I'm supposed to get 35 dollars."

He responded, "And you're right. But Erica made seven As too, and I can't afford to shell out 70 dollars. So I reduced your rewards down to 2 dollars per A."

I couldn't believe my daddy. Our rewards added together wouldn't even equal the amount that Daddy would have paid me if Erica was not living with us. I was upset, but I had to look like I understood. I didn't want Daddy to take the 14 dollars that I did have.

Erica was standing in the doorway the whole time with this silly look on her face, as if she was pleased with herself. I didn't even acknowledge her. I just went into my room and started on my homework.

Seconds later, I heard a knock on the door. Erica wanted to come in to talk. I was about to tell her to go find a new place to live, but I remembered that Mama asked me to be nice. "Come in," I said through clenched teeth.

Erica came in and sat down on my bed.

"What's up?"

Erica began. "This moment is so bitter-sweet," she said.

I agreed. This moment would have been sweeter if I could've gotten my 35 dollars.

"This is the first time that I ever made straight As. And my mom's not even here to see it."

Erica started crying. I couldn't imagine what life would be like if one of my parents died. Suddenly, I got sad too.

"I know your mother is in Heaven, and I know she's proud of you," I said. I didn't really know if I was right. But those words seemed to best fit the situation.

Erica wiped her tears. "I know you think that I'm bad, but I'm not. I'm only like this because of the things I've been through. And it just seems like things keep getting worse."

I stared at Erica for a while. Then I grabbed her hand and held it tight. I knew the feeling. I was experiencing it right then.

"People say that things get better after a while," I said. Then I added, "Now, I don't know if that's the truth, but that's what people say."

Erica laughed. "Well, I hope it's the truth because I'm tired of all of this heartache," she said, while leaving the room.

As I did my homework, I smiled. Mama had told me that I could get along with Erica, but I was so busy looking at how different she was that I was unwilling to figure out how we could get along. I made a silent vow to look at her in a more positive way.

That vow, however, was quickly forgotten at dinnertime. We were all sitting at the dinner table—enjoying Mama's meatloaf—when my father made an announcement: "Erica, we know your birthday is in three weeks, and your Auntie and I were thinking about throwing you a Sweet Sixteen. How does that sound?"

I almost choked on my mashed potatoes.

"That sounds crazy to me," I said. My mother stared at me as if she regretted the day that she pushed me out of her stomach.

"Ashley, we were talking to Erica," she said.

I threw my napkin down. "Well since I am no longer a part of this family," I said, "then perhaps I should excuse myself from the table."

My mother jumped up, reached across the table, and grabbed the front of my shirt. "Who do you think you are talking to?" she asked with an eerie calmness. I wanted to respond, but I was too shocked. As mad as Mama has been with me, she has never snatched my shirt. I guess she forgot that money didn't grow on trees that day.

My daddy calmed her down. "Alicia, let her go. I understand why Ashley's upset. She's not used to having her cousin here and now she has to share everything."

Mama let my shirt go, and I finally exhaled.

Erica responded. "Thank you so much for the offer, but I don't want to start any drama.

I don't need a party." Erica looked at me when she said the word "drama."

"There won't be any drama because everyone at this table agrees that you deserve a party," Mama said. She looked at me when she said "everyone." I swallowed hard.

After washing the dishes and sweeping the kitchen, I went into my parents' room to talk. Mama must have also been waiting for me because she started in on me as soon as I opened the door.

"Ashley," she said, "What you did at the kitchen table was so rude."

Mama opened a can of worms with that statement. She didn't realize that I was ready to go to battle.

"Mama, I feel like the party invitation was rude." Daddy sat straight up in the bed. "I have been a part of this family for eleven years, and you have never thrown me a party. How do you think that made me feel?"

I was anxious to see how she was going to work her way out of this one.

"Ashley, each year we have asked you what you wanted for your birthday. When you were five, you asked for a pet fish, and we got you an entire aquarium. When you turned eight, you asked us to take you to Disney World, and we did. We have consistently done what you wanted us to do. If you wanted a party, all you had to do was ask."

Mama may have thought that she made a good point, but I had an even better one: "First of all, all those fish died."

Mama rolled her eyes.

"And secondly, Erica didn't have to ask for a party. You offered."

Daddy decided to come to Mama's rescue on this one. He looked at me and said, "Erica isn't our child, so she probably didn't know that she *could* ask. You are our child. You should understand that if you ask for something and we have the ability to give it to you, we will. I don't expect to have to offer you anything because you should already know that you can have it."

For the first time in my life, I was completely speechless. My parents actually had a better point than the one I had.

Before I turned away, though, I decided to test my parents. "I would like to make a request, then," I said.

"What is it that you want?" Mama asked.

"I would like you to help me make some friends." Before I knew it, the tears started falling. "I'm getting so tired of sitting at a lunch table with people I barely know—all because I can't sit with anyone else because it's against an unwritten cafeteria rule. I'm tired of having to defend myself all the time because people are making fun of me. And I'm tired of fighting with Erica!"

My parents' mouths dropped open. "What are you talking about?" Daddy asked.

In thirty seconds, words spewed out of my mouth like vomit. I told my parents about everything—about how the cafeteria was divided by race, about how I had no friends, about how the cool girls have continued to tease me each day, and about how I was frustrated with Erica. "The only peaceful place I have is this house, and now I have to share my family with Cousin It!"

Mama ran to me and hugged me tightly. "I'm so sorry, Ashley. I know this is a hard time for you, and we haven't really checked to see if you were okay."

"I'm sorry too, Pumpkin," Daddy said. "We'll try our best to make sure you get some peace in your life."

As I walked back to my room, I felt lighter—as if a great weight had been lifted from my shoulders. I didn't know how, but I knew deep down inside that I would be able to survive this year—one way or another.

STEP EIGHT:

Don't Let Sleeping Dogs Lie

By the first week in November, a sense of normalcy returned to my school life. I had finally memorized the routines in each class, and I had finally discovered what would please my teachers. I was making awesome grades, and I was getting to know more kids in my classes. Lunch was even getting better. The cool girls finally stopped making rude comments when I walked by. Mama had told me not to ignore my problems, but it seemed that ignoring those girls had worked. The cafeteria was still divided, but no one was bothering me anymore. I was happier than I had been in months.

The happiness didn't last though. On Tuesday of that week, Mrs. James had called on a kid named Joshua to answer a simple question in math class: "Joshua, what's one-fourth times two-eighths?"

The entire class watched as Joshua held up his fingers and started counting. "4, 8, 12." Then he looked at Mrs. James and said with confidence: "The answer is 12!"

Mrs. James was usually always prepared. She knew math like the back of her hand, and she always had a way of steering a lost child in the right direction. But as the class stared at her, we immediately knew that she was the lost child in this case.

"How did you get that answer?" Mrs. James asked, while scratching her head.

"One-fourth times two-eighths is 12 because... because..." Joshua turned red. He stared at everyone else. We watched as his knees started shaking. He then looked down at the floor and refused to answer.

For a good minute, everyone was silent. Including me. I tried to stifle the laughter that I felt forming in my belly, but it continued to climb up my body until it reached my throat. All of a sudden, it poured out of me. It couldn't be tamed.

I wasn't trying to laugh, but his response sounded ridiculous. I laughed so hard that I couldn't breathe.

The rest of the class began laughing after my cue. Joshua was so upset that he had to excuse himself from the classroom. When he returned, the class had already stopped laughing and was taking notes from the lesson. I thought that the situation was over, but as soon as the bell rang for lunch, I found a group of angry kids surrounding me in the courtyard. I recognized some of them from the cool kids' tables. Joshua was the ringleader.

"You want to laugh at something," one of them said, "Then laugh at this."

The speaker threw a rock at me. I knew I could take her on her own, but I wasn't sure if I could handle five kids at the same time. So, I just opted to talk trash.

"If you could really fight, you wouldn't need to throw rocks." I wanted her to drop her handful of stones, but she kept them clenched in her fists.

All of a sudden, I saw Blondie walk up to us. She was staring in disbelief. "What in the world is going on here?" she asked.

Joshua decided to answer her. "This Black girl had the whole class laughing at me in English class." He didn't actually use the phrase "Black girl." In reality, he called me the "N" word. I exploded.

"I'll show you!" I said as I charged at him. I threw a punch, and the girl who threw rocks was about to hit me, but Blondie stopped her.

"Caitlin," she said. "Don't hit her back. If you do, you'll be acting just like her. Daddy told us that we're better than her kind anyway." The girl put her fist down and dropped the rocks just before my math teacher walked up.

"What's going on here?" Mrs. James asked. I began to explain, but Joshua beat me to it. "

"She hit me in my face out of nowhere," he lied.

I started trembling. "I hit him because he called me the "N" word!"

"Does this have anything to do with what happened in math class?" Mrs. James asked. I looked at Joshua, and he put his head down. Shaking her head, Mrs. James grabbed both Joshua and my hands and walked us to the principal's office. Joshua's crew followed.

After thirty minutes of heated debate and red faces, Dr. Johnson called our parents. He told them that they needed to pick us up from school because we were both in trouble. Joshua was sentenced to one day of in-school suspension, and I was sentenced to three days of out-of-school suspension since I had hit him.

Perhaps the most shocking thing of it all was when our parents arrived. The same man who arrived for Blondie before also came for Joshua. I then realized that Blondie and Joshua were siblings. It turned out that Caitlin was Blondie's sister as well.

Mama needed a better explanation as to why Joshua and I had different consequences. The principal explained to her that Joshua didn't touch me, and he also said that this was my second serious offense.

I interjected. "But Mama, Caitlin was throwing rocks at me," I said. The principal looked at Mama and said, "No one else will corroborate that story." Mama lowered her head.

Blondie's father wanted to know what sparked the whole argument.

"Your son answered a math question wrong, and Ashley laughed at him. Your son was embarrassed and confronted her after class. Apparently, he used some colorful language in the discussion, and Ashley got upset."

"Well, what did he say?" my mother asked. I was glad that she asked.

"He called me the "N" word, Mama," I said. "And apparently he is being taught that white people are better than Black people at home because his sister seems to think that they are better than us."

Mama looked at the principal. Dr. Johnson responded, "I am not responsible for what is being taught at home, ma'am. All I am responsible for is seeing that our students are able to learn in a *nonviolent* environment." He emphasized the word "nonviolent" and looked at me.

Mama could barely contain her anger. She jumped up.

"Are you serious? I have taught my daughter to treat people equally. The only time she has ever been in trouble at this school is when she felt like she had to protect herself from kids like this." She pointed at Blondie's siblings. "Racist comments are a type of violence. How is she supposed to feel after someone calls her the "N" word?"

Joshua's father spoke. "She should feel normal. After all, Black people call other Black people the "N" word. Why should she get all upset if someone else decides to use it?"

He said this statement with a smile, but no one else could see what was funny.

My mother turned around to address him. "There are a few problems with your logic. First of all, these Black people do not call other Black people that word. Number two, my daughter's name is not the "N" word. The only name anyone should ever use when addressing her is Ashley. And number three, you aren't Black. So you shouldn't be concerned with what other Black people do to other Black people."

Joshua's father's smile evaporated.

Mama went on to warn the principal that if he didn't educate the entire school about racism, then she would go to every news organization in Central Florida with this story. Dr. Johnson obliged.

When the meeting was over, I was scared. I thought I would surely get in trouble, but when I told Mama that I was sorry for hitting the boy, she looked at me with confusion.

"Ashley, you should have knocked his teeth out." Then on second thought, she said, "Wait a minute, let me be clear. Violence is not cool. But if Dr. Johnson thought I was going to allow someone to degrade you without coming to your defense, he had another thing coming."

She took a deep breath and then decided to take a moment to rub in that she was right. "See what I told you? These people that you go to school with have their own notions about who Black people are and what they do. Never in a million years would I have actually thought that my daughter would have to go through some of the same things that I went through." She started to cry.

I rubbed her shoulder to console her. "Mama, it's okay. I know who I am. I know I'm not an "N" word."

Mama wiped her eyes and said, "I know, baby. But everyone is not like you. I do a lot of people's hair, and you would be surprised to see how many children there are who still don't know that they are beautiful. They hate their hair, their skin tone, and they hate their features because someone lied to them and told them that they were not good enough or pretty enough. Someone told them that being Black is bad, and they believed them. I'm not just going to sit down on this experience, Ashley. I'm going to do something about it."

For the rest of the ride home, I silently wondered what my mother would do. I knew that she was capable of anything. I also knew one thing for sure: whatever it was, no one would forget it!

STEP NINE:

Look At Difference As A Good Thing

Students piled into the auditorium and sat in the chairs. We were cooped together like sardines in a can. I surveyed the room looking for familiar faces. In the row behind me, I spotted Ben and Tasha. Their faces brightened when they saw me.

"Do you know why we're here?" Ben asked me. He had to yell above the rest of the voices.

I yelled back. "No clue!"

I didn't think any of the students in the auditorium knew why they were there. The only thing we were told was that there was an emergency school meeting, and it was mandatory that every student attended. Truth is, I didn't really care about why I was there. All I knew was that this was my opportunity to miss Study Hall, so I was okay with anything that was about to happen.

A hush came over the auditorium as Dr. Johnson walked out onto the stage. He was wearing a pin-stripe suit with a bright red tie. He looked very distinguished, but I could tell he was nervous. Beads of sweat had collected on his forehead. He cleared his throat before leaning forward into the microphone.

"Good afternoon, Live Oak," he started. "I'm sure that most of you are confused about why you're here."

"We sure are," someone shouted from the audience. People started laughing, but then

Dr. Johnson gave us all his famous "Don't Try It" look and the auditorium immediately grew silent.

"Well, you're here to discuss a very important issue." He stopped to take a breath, and then he continued. "Recently, a parent asked me if I would want to be a student at this school. And I said 'No.' I would not want to come here everyday, and I certainly wouldn't feel as if I were a part of this community."

A gasp could be heard sweeping throughout the auditorium. Tasha turned and looked at me. We could not believe our ears. Dr. Johnson continued.

"You see, I don't know if you've noticed it, but I have a large gap in between my front teeth." He smiled so that we could see it. "It's big. But I never truly noticed it until recently because no one has ever really brought it to my attention. See, I went to an all-boys boarding school when I was your age. And I grew up with the same boys for years. Most of my friends were just like me. We liked to play ball together, and we liked to watch the same types of movies, and we were even interested in the same types of hobbies. So they never thought it necessary to point out that I had a gap. As a matter of fact, I don't even know if they noticed my gap."

He stopped and looked around the room. He wanted his words to sink in. I silently wondered what his point was.

"It was only when I started working with a diverse staff that I began to compare myself to others. It was when I saw Mrs. James's perfect teeth that I realized mine were flawed."

I took a second to look at Mrs. James, who was standing by the auditorium doors. She blushed and covered her mouth in surprise. Dr. Johnson continued.

"It was when I looked at Mr. Manor that I realized I was short for a guy."

Dr. Johnson was right. Mr. Manor was over 6 feet tall. Dr. Johnson's head came to Mr. Manor's shoulder. *But, what was his point?*

"You see, difference can be a good and beautiful thing. But it can also cause you to be self-conscious about the things that make you different—like your skin color, or the way that you speak, or even the way that you walk."

I thought about Erica. We were the definition of different. We talked differently, we dressed differently, we had completely different hairstyles, and we had a completely different way of looking at things. And these differences have caused us to argue and fight with each other. *But was Dr. Johnson implying that we could get along—even though we were so different?*

Dr. Johnson's speech resumed.

"In the past few weeks, I've seen too many conflicts in this school—and they all stem from difference. I've seen students calling each other derogatory names. I've seen groups of students surrounding and attacking other students who didn't look like them. I've even seen people refuse to sit with other students just because they are a different race. The entire cafeteria is segregated. No one wants to talk to, hang out with, or befriend anyone who is different from them. And this has to stop."

Dr. Johnson said the last part with emphasis. I looked around the auditorium. Everyone sat completely still.

"I know that you all have heard me repeat constantly that you should treat others the way you want to be treated. And I know you've heard me preach to you that it's important to respect each other—no matter how different another person may be. But it's still not happening. And frankly, I'm tired of all the drama that you are bringing to this school."

He pointed at the entire room. I was confused. *How was I bringing drama to this school*, I thought. *I'm the victim in this entire situation.*

"So, rather than continuing to preach at you," Dr. Johnson said, "I decided to ask someone else to come to speak with you today. Maybe if you heard what she had to say, you would change your ways. Maybe you would start treating others with respect. And maybe, just maybe, this would finally become the school that I would want to attend."

My mind started racing. Dr. Johnson always did all the "building community" speeches in the school. *So who did he bring in to talk to us about this?* I took a second to look around the room. All of the teachers were looking surprised—as if they hadn't heard of the guest speaker. *Who was this mystery woman?*

Dr. Johnson spoke. "The woman that I'm bringing before you has worked in a profession that has brought her into contact with many different people. And, after talking to her, you would never guess that she has been a victim of racism herself. Her story is quite compelling, and if you listen carefully, I have no doubt that you will completely change the way you look at other people. So, without further ado, I introduce to you: Mrs. Alicia Woods!"

As I watched my mother walk out on the stage, my mouth dropped open. *WHAT IN THE PEANUT BUTTER AND PICKLE SANDWICH IS GOING ON HERE*? I thought.

I wanted to scream.

STEP TEN:

Never Underestimate Your Mom

Mrs. Woods, also known as my mother, walked quickly across the stage and stepped up to the microphone. I was in complete and utter shock. Not only did she neglect to mention she would be coming to my school today, but she also neglected to consult me on the outfit she should wear. I watched in total embarrassment as my mom—dressed in a bright yellow shirt and black slacks—started to speak. She looked like a giant lemon wedge.

"Hello, Live Oak," she said. The rest of the kids responded by saying "Hello." I stayed silent. I was too busy repeating the phrase "Please don't embarrass me... please don't embarrass me..." in my head.

"For those of you who don't know me," she continued, "I'm Ashley's mom. Hi, Ashley!!!!" she yelled as she cupped her hands over her eyes and stared into the audience. She was trying to find me, but the bright spotlight she was standing under on the stage blocked her vision. I wanted to be a good sport and say "Hey, Mama," but I couldn't. I was completely frozen. I actually wanted to die.

"Well, she's shy," my mom continued. "I promise I won't embarrass you, baby girl," she said. "Anyway, I'm so excited to be here. I've always wanted to help your generation accomplish great things, and this is the first step. So thank you so much for coming here and listening to what I have to say."

At this, some kids in the auditorium clapped, and a couple of kids sitting next to me nudged me. It was their sign of approval. It made me feel a little better, but I was still angry. She could've told me she was making her debut motivational speech at MY school.

"I am a hairstylist," my mother said. "I used to style everyone's hair in my neighborhood when I was your age. At that time, I would braid people's hair. All the girls in my neighborhood had the latest styles and they loved me. They would tell their friends, and then they would tell their friends, and before I knew it, business was booming! I was the only eleven-year-old in the entire neighborhood with over two thousand dollars saved from all the money I earned from doing people's hair. I had planned to use that money to help me get my first car. I figured that by the time I was sixteen, I would have 6 thousand dollars, and I could buy the car flat-out with some money left over."

Mama took a second, swallowed, and then resumed her speech. "Now, everyone in my neighborhood was Black. But I didn't go to an all-Black junior high school. My mom wanted my sister and me to get a better education than the kind I could get in my neighborhood. So, when I went to middle school, I went to the "white" school that was on the other side of town. And although there were some other Black students there, the school had far more white students. Suddenly I was placed in a totally different environment than I was at my previous school. And it didn't take long to realize I was different."

I could feel the change in my mother's voice. She had started out her speech with so much hope and conviction, but her voice suddenly became sad. *What happened to her at that school*, I wondered. *And why hasn't she told me this story before?*

"At first, my sister and I were teased because of our dark skin tone. They would call us Midnight 1 and Midnight 2. And they loved comparing us to monkeys. But one day, my sister got angry and started bragging about all the money I had from doing other people's hair. She told them, "It doesn't matter how Black she is; she has more green than all of y'all." And that made those white kids so mad."

I looked around the room. Everyone was tuned into my mother. They wanted to know what happened next. I hated to admit it, but so did I.

"So one day, they asked me to prove it. They told me to bring the money to school so that they could see it. They said, 'If you show us the money, we won't tease you ever again. We won't call you a monkey anymore because monkeys don't have money.' I should've been smarter. I should've known those kids were up to no good, but I was so eager for the teasing to stop that I decided to give them what they wanted. So, the next day, I put my money shoebox in my book-bag, and I brought all of my money to school. At that time, I had 2,065 dollars in that shoebox."

My mom's voice broke. She sounded as if she were about to cry. I started to tear up as well.

"Sure enough, when my sister and I showed them the money, they got angry, pushed us down to the ground, and started to kick and punch us. They were yelling at the top of their lungs the whole entire time. They said, "Monkeys shouldn't have money." They told me they would make sure I never had money again. And then they took my money. And they said if we told anyone, they would come to our house and hurt our whole family. They beat us so bad that I could barely get up after the incident, and they knocked out one of my sister's teeth."

Sniffles echoed throughout the auditorium. Several students and teachers were crying. My heart was completely broken. I could not believe that my mother had gone through something like this.

"The worst part of it all," she continued, "was that there were other kids watching the entire time. And they didn't do a thing about it. They didn't try to stop those kids, they didn't tell an adult. They just let those kids beat us and steal my money."

She paused.

"When my sister and I got up off that floor, we were never the same again. My sister was angry. She was so angry that she hated white people completely. When we had to go to the doctor, she refused to let a white doctor treat her. She stopped going to stores run by white people, and she refused to work with or even converse with white people. She even replaced her tooth with a gold implant because she thought gold teeth was a "Black people" thing."

Mom continued. "I was angry too, but I responded in a different way. I decided that

I had to become my best self so that I could break through the limits that ignorant people had imposed on me. So, I continued to do hair, but I learned how to do all types of hair so that I could make more money. I went to business school so that I could learn how to run a successful business. And I devoted all of my time and energy to becoming excellent. My excellence has allowed me to style a variety of different hair types, and it has even allowed me to style celebrity hair. I've done Dakota Tremon's hair and I've also styled Marxie Powers' hair."

The room erupted in applause. The kids were impressed that Mom knew Dakota and Marxie—both teen idols who had their own television shows and YouTube channels. I was impressed for a different reason. I was proud of my mom for turning the bitter incident that she had experienced into an opportunity to grow. If I had gone through something like that, I would've probably burned the school down and been on my way to jail.

"People who know my story always ask me if I hate those kids for what they did to me and my sister. And the truth is, I don't. Those kids—as mean and ugly as they were—were just ignorant. They were so focused on our differences that they didn't realize we were very similar. Those kids had siblings—just like my sister and I were siblings. They wanted to get an education and do something with their lives just like my sister and I did. They went to the same school as we did, and they were human beings just like us. Both of us had blood coursing through our veins, and we all had insecurities. We were all human beings. The differences—our skin color, our background, and where we lived—were all just small parts of us. So they should not have been a big deal. Instead, we should have focused on our similarities, and we would have gotten along just fine."

"And so I say the same thing to you: stop focusing on each other's differences. Once you realize that we are all really more of the same than we are different, you will grow a new respect for one another, and school will become a much more rewarding experience. You will stop picking on each other. You will stop fighting with one another, and you will recognize each other as you are—a beautiful melting pot of strong, talented, gifted, and intelligent individuals."

People started applauding again. I joined in too. My mom's speech was great.

"Now, before I go, I want to be clear. In order for this change to happen, you have to work hard to ensure that you and others are treating people fairly. You cannot be like those bystanders who allowed those mean kids to beat my sister and me up. You have to take a stand. So you have homework."

I spoke too soon. My mom's speech *was* great—until she mentioned homework.

"Next week, you must sit with people at lunch time who are clearly different from you and you must talk with them. You must do this for the entire week—all five days."

People started groaning. Teachers started shushing. And my mother continued.

"Then, you must make sure you stop anyone who is making fun of someone else or treating them unfairly. It is your job to be sure that this school becomes one that truly celebrates difference. Teachers will be on the lookout for students who are really upholding our standards, and they will be shouted out for their excellence.

The room quieted down immediately. I could tell the kids liked the "shout out" part.

"Because I love you guys and am so committed to you being the best school in America, this will be a continual conversation. We will set aside time on a monthly basis to talk about difference and to try to understand each other. I look forward to seeing you soon. Good luck and remember, we are more the same than we are different!"

Everyone stood and clapped as my mom left the stage. I couldn't believe it, but my clapping was loudest of all.

STEP ELEVEN:

Realize That Change is Hard

"How come you never told *me* that story?" I asked my mom as we left the school. "And why didn't you tell me you were coming to school today?"

"Oh, Ashley," Mama said, "It wasn't something you needed to know until now. And I don't have to tell you everything, do I?"

"Actually, yes you do," I snapped. "I could've helped you pick out your outfit."

"Girl, please," Mama said, "This outfit is fly."

We rode in silence during the ride home. I was thinking about my Mom. I wondered how she could be so pleasant and nice after experiencing something so toxic. And I silently wondered if her speech would really make a difference. Would Blondie, Joshua, and their sister stop glaring at me every time they saw me around the school? Would the students really start sitting with different people in the cafeteria? And would Erica and I be able to make it through one afternoon without arguing? I didn't know, but I knew that these changes wouldn't come about easily.

I broke the silence. "Mama, I really hope all of these kids listen to you. They need to wake up and treat people better."

Mama stared at the road with a puzzled look on her face. "These kids? What about *you*?" she asked.

"What *about* me?" I quickly retorted. I was completely innocent in this whole situation. I couldn't help it if some stuck up kids decided that they were going to attack me and call me names. I couldn't help being Black. *What did Mama want from me?*

"Ashley, you have played a big role in everything that has happened to you."

Suddenly, I was all-ears. "Mama, what are you talking about?"

Mama drove into the Publix parking lot and parked the car. *Uh oh*, I thought.

She turned to me. "Ashley, I realized something today. I've been so busy taking up for you that I've made you think that you were completely innocent. But you're not."

My eyes popped open in disbelief. How could my mom blame me for the way these kids have been treating me?

"Just like those people at school, you have judged things and people based on how they look!" she said.

"Oh, Mama, that's ridiculous!"

"Is it? Ashley, the whole reason you wanted to go to this school is because it looked so beautiful on the outside. You didn't even bother to ask any questions, do any research, or get to know any of the teachers or kids here before making your decision."

"Mama-" I tried to interject. She cut me off.

"I'm not finished. You also said the blonde girl hit you with her ponytail on purpose, but from the way she described it in that apology note, she didn't even realize she hit you."

"You read the note?" I asked. I had folded that note and tucked it in my bottom desk drawer. I was confused about how she found it. "Mama, what about my privacy?"

"Little girl, you have no privacy in my house," Mama said.

"So, what was I supposed to do? Just let her embarrass me in front of everyone?"

"No, Ashley. I'm not telling you to just let people disrespect you. I'm telling you to try to understand people so you can respond appropriately. If you knew that she had accidently hit you with her ponytail, would you have grabbed it and thrown her on the floor? Or would you have handled it differently?

Mama looked at me. Truth was, I didn't know.

"And what about Erica? You still aren't getting along with her—after months."

"I can't get along with her. She talks too much. She tries to take over our dinner conversation everyday, and that's the only time we all sit and talk. She knows how I feel about that, and she's still doing it on purpose."

The tears started pouring down my face. I couldn't believe Mama was telling me I was wrong when all of these people were intentionally trying to ruin my life.

Mama spoke with a gentler voice. "Ashley, I loved my sister dearly, but motherhood was not her first priority. She was busy all the time, so

Auntie Sarah didn't treat Erica the same way Daddy and I treat you. I know for a fact that she didn't have dinnertime conversations with Erica."

She paused to wipe my tears away, and then she continued speaking. "So, she's probably talking so much because-"

I finished Mama's sentence. "because she's so happy to have someone to talk to."

Mama nodded, and I started thinking about what she was saying.

"And what about Joshua?" Mama asked. "You laughed at him. Was that nice?"

"Mama, his answer was ridiculous!"

"It was ridiculous to you because you're strong in math. But everyone is not like you! What if he has a learning disability in math? Or what if his last three math teachers were horrible? Would you have still laughed at him if you knew his story?"

I shook my head.

"You're wondering why people are angry with you and why you can't find peace in your life, but you haven't done one thing to get to know anyone. When you see other people's flaws, you laugh at them, or try to pull them down so that you can feel better about yourself. But you never take time to actually understand them. Ashley, everyone—including you—has a story."

Mama had my complete attention.

"The only reason Daddy and I get along is because I know my flaws. That keeps me humble when I'm dealing with him. I'm clumsy and he's lazy at times. I don't get upset when he doesn't do the dishes because I remember those times I broke dishes and he helped me clean it up. If you want to build real relationships with people and stop letting silly things—like race—get in the way, you're going to have to understand that you are imperfect too. And then you'll be ready to really make a change at your school."

I hated to admit it, but Mama was right. I knew I had work to do, but I didn't even know where to start.

Luckily, Mama had the answer.

"Next week, I want you to do your best to get to know some of the kids that sit at that table."

"The cool kids' table?" I asked.

"Yes—that's the one."

"But Mama-"

"But nothing," she said. "I want you to find some things you have in common with them. Then, everyday, I want you to come home and give Erica a compliment. Maybe then you will discover that you had friends around you this entire time."

She started the car and pulled out of the parking lot. We finished the rest of the drive in silence, but my mind was going a mile a minute. Having to compliment Erica—that's one thing. Having to converse with the kids at the cool table—that's another thing. I was really starting to think I wouldn't survive sixth grade.

STEP TWELVE:

Remember That Everyone Has a Story

When the lunch bell rang, I walked slowly to the cafeteria. It was Monday—the first day of Mama's challenge. People had already seemed to be acting nicer to each other, but lunch would be the real test. And I was not looking forward to it.

With each step, I was reminding myself of the vow I had made the night before: that no matter what, I would follow Mama's directions.

By the time I made it to the door, I had convinced myself that the cafeteria would no longer be segregated. But when I walked into the cafeteria, it looked exactly the same as any other day. Everyone was sitting in the seats in which they always sat. The cool girls were still all seated at their tables; the Black kids were seated at their tables. I spotted Tasha and Brittany at my table and stopped to speak to them.

"Why are you guys still sitting here? You know we're supposed to be trying to sit with other people this week," I said.

Brittany looked at me. "Girl, I know that's what your mom told us to do, but what's the point? Nothing's going to change."

Tasha nodded her head in agreement. "Yeah girl. This school has been like this, and we're new. We can't change this system by ourselves."

I opened up my lunchbox. "Well, I'm going to try," I said. Then I changed the subject. "My mom bought a whole box of Takis for me so that

I could share with kids at school and make some friends." I pulled out two packs. "Do you want some?"

Brittany and Tasha grabbed the packs.

"Of course we do," Brittany said.

I spotted Ben in the Hispanic section and started heading in his direction. He was talking to his other friends, but when he saw me, he smiled.

"Hi, Ben," I said when I had reached his table. I took four packs of Takis out, and I turned to the rest of the kids at the table. "I don't know if you guys even like these, but feel free to have some."

"Thanks!" Ben said. "My friend Miguel loves these."

Miguel turned to me. "I'm Miguel, by the way," he said.

"Hi, Miguel. I'm-"

"Ashley," he interrupted. "I'm pretty sure the entire school knows your name."

I giggled. "Yeah, my mom put me on the spot."

One of the other kids at the table grabbed a bag and popped a Taki into his mouth. "Did you know your mom was coming on Friday?" he asked.

"I had no idea," I said. "She totally surprised me."

Ben put his hand on mine. "Thanks for the snacks, Ashley," he said. "Would you like to sit down?"

I looked over at Blondie's table. Blondie was sitting there—along with her sister, Caitlin, and about seven other girls. I couldn't prove it, but it felt like they were talking about me. I didn't want to sit with them. But I couldn't disappoint my mama.

"Um... I can't," I said to Ben. "This challenge was my mom's idea, and no one is doing it. I have to be the one to break the ice."

I picked up my lunchbox and walked to the cool kids' table. I felt as if I were walking the plank.

When I arrived, all the girls stopped talking and stared at me.

I spoke directly to Blondie. "Can I talk to you for a second?"

She looked at her friends. Some of them shook their heads.

"You can talk," she said. Her words were icy cold.

"I was hoping that we could speak alone."

She looked at her friends again then shook her head. "Anything you have to say can be said right here."

The old me would have gotten angry. But something was happening to me.

Calmly, I said: "I just wanted to apologize. I realized I played a role in the drama we are having with each other. I was angry with you for calling me a racist name, so when your ponytail hit me, I just assumed you did it on purpose. But you probably didn't even realize that had happened."

Blondie's expression softened. "You're right. I didn't even realize that calling you "Chia Pet" was racist in the first place. But I should've-"

Her sister, Caitlin, interrupted her. "You should've done exactly what you did. You didn't do anything wrong." Then she looked at me. "Can you leave please? We don't want to talk to you or anyone that looks like you."

I was about to pounce on her like a cat, but someone grabbed my shoulder just as I was about to leap.

"Ashley, is there a problem here?"

I turned around. Ben was holding my shoulder with a firm grip. His face was tight with anger.

Caitlin started laughing. "Oh no," she said. "Don't tell me that this kid is your bodyguard."

The whole table started laughing.

Caitlin continued. "You can't fight your own battles? You need *this chico* to do it for you?"

All of a sudden, I couldn't take it anymore. I ran out of the cafeteria. Tears poured down my face as I ran into the bathroom, closed the stall, and locked the door. I hated everything and everyone. I was mad at my mom for starting this stupid challenge, and I was angry with Ben for trying to defend me. Mostly, though, I was angry with myself. I should've listened to Brittany and Tasha when they said that things would never change in my school. I should've known that no apology could erase the drama that I had gotten myself into. This was just the way it was, and I was going to have to accept it.

Just as I was about to leave the stall, I heard a faint knock on the door. I stepped out of the stall and saw Blondie staring at me. Her face was red, but it was kind.

"I'm so sorry for what just happened," she said. "My sister is an idiot. And I just told her that in front of the whole cafeteria."

I knew I was mad, *but were my ears playing tricks on me*?

"She's still upset about what happened to us," she said.

"What happened?" I asked, as I wiped the tears from my cheeks.

"A few months ago, a Black guy robbed my mom at gunpoint, and my mom hasn't been the same. She started being afraid to go out at night, and then she started being afraid to leave the house at all. My dad was so upset that he wasn't there to defend her, and now-"

She started crying.

"Now, we've become... this," she said.

I knew what she was talking about. Because of that incident, her family started thinking that every Black person was bad. And even though I was still frustrated with what happened in the cafeteria, I was actually glad she shared this with me.

"Well," I said, "My mom pointed out that I have a problem understanding people. So, I guess we've both got a lot of work to do."

For some reason, we started giggling.

"I'm too embarrassed to leave this restroom," I said. "Do you think I can stay in here forever?"

She smiled at me. "Don't be like my mom," she said. "Let's face the music together.

Just then, the bell rang to signal the end of lunch. And just as the kids poured out of the cafeteria, Blondie grabbed my arm, wrapped her hand around mine, and held on tight.

We walked out the bathroom—Black and white—together.

STEP THIRTEEN:

If All Else Fails, Dance

"Ashley, go get the door!" Mama yelled. She was carrying a tray of vegetables in one hand, and a tray of plastic wine glasses full of sparkling grape juice in the other.

Aloud, I said: "Okay, Mama." But to myself I said: *Where's Erica? Why can't she answer the door?*

I was tired. I had spent the entire morning scrubbing down the house and helping Mama make barbecue chicken and mac-and-cheese—all while Erica took one hundred years to get ready. I barely wanted Erica to have this party anyway, and now Mama wanted me to play hostess? This was too much.

The only part of this night that made me excited was the fact that Erica allowed me to invite my friends too. Brittany and Tasha had already arrived earlier. So, it wasn't a surprise when I opened the door and saw Ben standing on the other side. What did surprise me, however, was the way Ben looked. He had dressed up for the occasion: he had on a collar shirt, slacks, and some dress shoes. This was a step up from the hat, jeans, and t-shirt look that I was sporting.

I couldn't contain my shock.

"Wow," I said when I opened the door. "Ben, you look fancy."

Ben smiled. "Can I come in?" he asked.

"Oh, sorry," I said as I gestured for him to come inside. And then I remembered what my mom told me to say to all guests upon their arrival. "Thank you for coming to Erica's Sweet Sixteen, and welcome to our humble abode!"

Ben looked around. His eyes were wide in amazement. "Your house is beautiful," he said. "I didn't know you were living like this."

I didn't think our house was that great, but I said, "Thanks, Ben!"

We walked into the family room. Daddy had moved the couch and the other furniture onto the patio so there was an open space. Erica, her friends, Brittany, and Tasha were standing in that open space now dancing to Drake's "In My Feelings." The color drained from my face as I watched Daddy hop on the dance floor like a chicken. He must've forgotten the only rule I set for him and Mama: no dancing!

Mama had just placed fresh cookies out on the table. When she saw Ben, she jogged to us with her arms wide open.

"Ben," Mama said. "You came!"

"Yes, Mrs. Woods. I wouldn't have missed this night for the world."

Mama looked him over. "I really like your 'fit," she said.

"Thanks, Mrs. Woods," he said.

Just then, the timer on the stove buzzed.

"The cupcakes are finished! Well, I'll leave you two. Have fun!" Mama hustled away.

Ben turned to me. "Want to dance?" he asked.

I started to say yes, but then the doorbell rang.

"I wonder who that could be," I said.

Ben joined the dance floor while I went to the front door. When I opened it, I gasped.

"Jenny, you came!" I said. I had forgotten that I had invited Jenny—also known as Blondie—to Erica's party. I had expected her to flake out, but she didn't.

"Of course I came. We're friends now. You do remember that, right?" Jenny asked while stepping inside.

I smiled. Ever since Jenny and I walked out of the restroom together, we had been cool. Jenny had even started sitting with Brittany, Tasha, Ben, and me at lunch. Her siblings weren't too happy about that, but she didn't seem to care.

"Where are Caitlin and Joshua?" I asked.

Jenny looked at me and frowned. "By now, you ought to know that they aren't cool with our friendship. They think I'm crazy to be your friend after everything that happened."

I closed the door. Jenny started walking toward the family room, but when she noticed I wasn't walking with her, she stopped and turned around.

"Why are you still standing there?" she asked.

I had a question for her. "Why *are* you my friend?"

She twisted up her face in confusion. "What?"

"You said your brother and sister think you're crazy for being my friend. So why did you decide to become my friend?"

"Oh," she said. "That's easy." She walked back toward me and looked me in my eyes. "It's because you didn't judge me. When I told you what I had been through, you listened. You didn't pressure me to think like you, you didn't tell me I was wrong, and you didn't get mad. You just listened."

She paused.

"All of my friends before you tried to pressure me to be exactly like them. My family wanted me to think just like they think. And that's why I was so mean to you when you came to our table that day. I wanted to please everyone else. And then I actually talked to you. You were the one person who should've been upset about my views, but instead of fighting, you just listened. You helped convince me that there are no good races and bad races; there are just simply good people and bad people. And the bad people come in every race, every shape, and every size."

She smiled.

"Anyone who can teach someone like me—who went through what I went through—that color doesn't matter can't be half bad."

She pulled my hand.

"Now, enough of this foolishness. I came here to have fun, and fun we shall have!"

I skipped down the hallway with her and entered the family room. Every single person at the party—my parents included—were on the dance floor screaming out "Keke, do you love me?"

Rather than join the party, I took a moment to survey the scene. Erica and her friends were doing the whole dance—as if they had studied the video. She had a big smile on her face. She must've felt my eyes on hers because she made eye contact with me and blew me a kiss. I never thought I would say this, but I was actually happy she came to live with us. Ever since I had been complimenting her, we had gotten along much better and even started getting close.

I caught her kiss and blew one back. Then I looked in the other direction.

Brittany, Tasha, Ben, and Jenny were dancing too. I was surprised at how much rhythm they had. They were doing their own dance moves to the song, but they almost looked choreographed.

And then I zoomed in on Jenny. She was the only white person at the party, but she didn't look uncomfortable. She was really just having fun, and I think it was because she was so free. She no longer cared about pleasing anyone. She just wanted to enjoy life to the fullest.

That's when I realized something. Mama said that you should learn things from everyone because everyone has a story. And maybe that's what I was supposed to learn from Jenny: life is more fun when you stop caring so much about what everyone else thinks.

I took my hat off and fluffed out my afro. Then, I joined Ben and Jenny and started dancing the night away. It was the most fun I had experienced in years.

Sixth grade wasn't so bad after all.

Made in the USA
Monee, IL
18 April 2024

57141920R00075